First World War
and Army of Occupation
War Diary
France, Belgium and Germany

1 INDIAN CAVALRY DIVISION
Headquarters, Branches and Services
Commander Royal Engineers
7 November 1914 - 28 February 1915

WO95/1169/1

The Naval & Military Press Ltd
www.nmarchive.com
Published in association with The National Archives

Published by

The Naval & Military Press Ltd

Unit 10 Ridgewood Industrial Park,

Uckfield, East Sussex,

TN22 5QE England

Tel: +44 (0) 1825 749494

www.naval-military-press.com

www.nmarchive.com

This diary has been reprinted in facsimile from the original. Any imperfections are inevitably reproduced and the quality may fall short of modern type and cartographic standards.

© **Crown Copyright**
Images reproduced by permission of The National Archives, London, England, 2015.

Contents

Document type	Place/Title	Date From	Date To
Heading	WO95/1169/1		
Heading	1 Indian Cav Div C R E 1914 Nov 1915 Feb		
Heading	War Diary of Indian C R E 1st Indian Cavalry Division From 7-11-14 To 30-11-14 Volume 1 1st To 3		
War Diary	Marseilles	07/11/1914	13/11/1914
War Diary	Orleans	15/11/1914	29/11/1914
War Diary	Auchel	30/11/1914	30/11/1914
Heading	War Diary of C.R.E 1st Indian Cavalry Divn From 3/12/14 To 31-12-14		
War Diary	Auchel	03/12/1914	08/12/1914
War Diary	Transfer Order for Col Baddeley were Received in evening.	09/12/1914	10/12/1914
War Diary	Auchel	10/12/1914	23/12/1914
War Diary	Hani	24/12/1914	25/12/1914
War Diary	St Hilaire	26/12/1914	31/12/1914
Heading	War Diary of Senior Engineer Officer 1st and Cavalry Division Form 1-1-1915 To 31-1-1915		
War Diary	War Diary of Senior Engineer Officer, 1st Indian Cavalry Division From 1st January 1915 To 31st January 1915		
War Diary	St. Hilaire	01/01/1915	31/01/1915
Heading	War Diary of Senior Royal Engineer Officer 1st Indian Cavalry Division From 1st February 1915 To 28th February 1915		
War Diary	St Hilaire	01/02/1915	28/02/1915

WO 95/1169/1

1 INDIAN CAV DIV

CRE

1914 NOV — 1915 FEB

War Diary
of Indian
C.R.E. 1st Cavalry Division

From 7-11-14
To 30-11-14

121/2143

Volume I

pp 1 to 3

{ WAR DIARY of INTELLIGENCE SUMMARY }

Instructions regarding War Diaries and Intelligence Summaries are contained in F. S. Regs., Part II, and the Staff Manual respectively. Title pages will be prepared in manuscript.

(Erase heading not required.)

Army Form O. 2118.

No 3 Section A. G's Office at Base I. E. Force
Passed to Genl. S. Sectn on 8-12-14

ADJUTANT GENERAL INDIA 846 W.D. -7. DEC 1914 BASE OFFICE

Hour, Date, Place.	Summary of Events and Information.	Remarks and references to Appendices.
7-11-14. MARSEILLES.	Head Qrs: Divl Engineers, 1st Indian Cavalry Division, arrived on H.T. "BALLARAT". (Strength as per column of remarks). Received information that the 1st Fd Troop (Mounted) had proceeded ahead with the 9th Cav. Brigade. EKS	H.Q. Cav. Divl. Engrs. Col. C.E. BADDELEY. Divl Eng. Comdr. Lt. Col. G.A. LESLIE. R.E. Major. A.G. BREMNER. R.E. Field Engineers.
10-11-14. —do—	2nd Fd Troop (Wheeled) arrived, disembarked, proceeded into camp at ST. MARCELLE. Col. LESLIE & Capt. SANDERS left by rail for ORLEANS, to enquire into & assist in arrangements for billetting & camps for the Division. EKS	Capt. A.R.C. SANDERS. R.E. " E.K.SQUIRES. R.E. Asst. F. E. S.Sergt. O'NEILL. Clerk. — EKS
13-11-14. —do—	Telegraphic orders received (thro' Ordnance, Communications) for drawing equipment & stores for 2nd Field Troops, which will bring them into line with Field Troops of British Expeditionary Force. EKS	
15-11-14. ORLEANS.	Remainder of H.Q. Cavl Divl Engineers arrived by rail from MARSEILLES. EKS	
16-11-14. —do—	2nd Field Troop arrived; proceeded into camp at LA SOURCE. OC. Field Troop instructed re. drawing of newly authorised equipment.	

WAR DIARY of INTELLIGENCE SUMMARY.

Army Form C. 2118.

(Erase heading not **required**.)

Hour, Date, Place.	Summary of Events and Information.	Remarks and references to Appendices.
16-11-14. (cont'd) ORLEANS.	Frost at night over the morning: orders issued to O.C. 2nd F. Troop to cover up exposed portions of pipe line at 2A SOURCE Camp. SKS	
21-11-14. —do—	2/Lt. WALLACK joined H.Q. Cav. Div. Eng'rs. as Interpreter. Lt.Col. LESLIE, Maj. BREMNER, Capt SANDERS and 2/Lt. WALLACK left ORLEANS by rail for Pt. of Assembly. Capt. E.K. SQUIRES appointed Staff Officer to Div. Eng'r Commander, with effect from 7-11-14. SKS	
22-11-14. —do—	O.C. 2 Fld. Troop ordered to furnish party to cover up exposed portions of pipe line at LES GRUES Camp. SKS	
24-11-14 —do—	No. 11. Motor-car (Sheffield-Simplex) received for use of Div. Eng. Com'r. Driver CATANEO, mechanic ANDRE. SKS	
26-11-14 —do—	Remainder of Div. Eng. H.Qrs. and the 2nd Field Troop entrained. SKS	
28-11-14 —do—	Detrained at LILLERS. Div. Eng. H.Qrs & the Field Troop billeted at AUCHEL. SKS	
29-11-14. —do—	Orders received for Capt SANDERS & Capt SQUIRES to report to G.O.C. Indian Army Corps. SKS	

WAR DIARY
or
INTELLIGENCE SUMMARY.

(Erase heading not required.)

Army Form C. 2118.

Instructions regarding War Diaries and Intelligence Summaries are contained in F. S. Regs., Part II, and the Staff Manual respectively. Title pages will be prepared in manuscript.

3

Hour, Date, Place.	Summary of Events and Information.	Remarks and references to Appendices.
30.11.14 AUCHEL	Captains Sanders & Squires reported departure for Indian Army Corps Hd. Qtr. on afternoon of 29.11.14. H.Q. 1. Cav. Div. informed. Lieut. Harris reported seriously ill and Lieut. Wickham asked for to replace him in the 2nd Field Troop. Col. Baddeley and Lieut. Col. Leslie went to St. Omer to interview A.A.G. for R.E. ALB C.M. Baddeley Colonel. Div. Eng. Comdr 1st Indian Cav. Div.	

War Diary
of
C.R.E. 1st Indian Cavalry Div

From 3/12/14
to 31.12.14

Volume ___

Pp ___ to ___

WAR DIARY
or
INTELLIGENCE SUMMARY.
(Erase heading not required.)

Army Form C. 2118.

Instructions regarding War Diaries and Intelligence Summaries are contained in F. S. Regs., Part II, and the Staff Manual respectively. Title pages will be prepared in manuscript.

Hour, Date, Place.	Summary of Events and Information.	Remarks and references to Appendices.
AUCHEL		
3 - 12 - 14	Colonels Baddeley & Leslie went to St Omer returning same day	A.9.B
4 - 12 - 14	Orders issued to collect material for sufficient to make up 1000 bombs and 500ˣ of bomb screens. Major Bremner was sent to Lillers & Ord. Rail head to collect wood and explosives.	A.9.B
5 - 12 - 14	Colonels Baddeley & Leslie visited the Chief Engineer I.A. Corps. They visited 2nd and 3rd line trenches etc. 2nd Field Troop made up 50 bombs. Major Bremner carried out experiments with bomb screens. Started trenches with civil labour.	A.9.B
6 - 12 - 14 -	Experiments in bomb screens. Major Bremner bought wood from Lillers & arranged for explosives to be supplied on 7-12-14. Lt. Col. Leslie reported departure for 3rd Ind. Divn. Field Troops employed on bombs - road repairs etc.	A.9.B

WAR DIARY
or
INTELLIGENCE SUMMARY.
(Erase heading not *required*.)

Army Form C. 2118.

Instructions regarding War Diaries and Intelligence Summaries are contained in F. S. Regs., Part II, and the Staff Manual respectively. Title pages will be prepared in manuscript.

Hour, Date, Place.	Summary of Events and Information.	Remarks and references to Appendices.
AUCHEL 7-12-14.	D.E.C. went to ST. OMER to see pumps, trench mortars etc. Lieut. WICKHAM, 2nd Field Troop reported arrival on afternoon. App. B	
8-12-14.	Experiments in tobacco tin bombs and bomb screens. Former successful. Latter proved that even 3 layers of wire netting often failed to repel a 5-lb. bomb – Expanded metal necessary. Issued 150 bombs to Ambala Brigade. On handing them over Captain MOLESWORTH gave only instruction in use of bombs that the men, up to that time, had received. Col. BADDELEY left to visit 1st line trenches. Asked H.Q. to obtain G.O.C's orders re. bomb screens. Visit to AIRE failed to produce any wire netting strong enough to keep out German bombs. Further instructions re. stables asked for – Also asked for a change in routine of work orders so that they would finally come from only one source.	Transfer orders for Col. BADDELEY were received in evening
9-12-14.		
10-12-14	Received orders not to put barbed wire on bomb screens & not to construct stables – Lt. Col. LESLIE returned from trenches. Col. BADDELEY's transfer orders were	

WAR DIARY
or
INTELLIGENCE SUMMARY.

(Erase heading not *required*.)

Army Form C. 2118.

Instructions regarding War Diaries and Intelligence Summaries are contained in F. S. Regs., Part II, and the Staff Manual respectively. Title pages will be prepared in manuscript.

Hour, Date, Place.	Summary of Events and Information.	Remarks and references to Appendices.
AUCHEL 10-12-14 (cont)	cut out to him. Col. BADDELEY returned at 6.00 p.m.	
11-12-14.	D.E.C. received orders for instruction in trench work being to Brigades. Visited Brigade Commanders and arranged to commence on 12.12.14. Col. BADDELEY left for LILLERS at 2.10 p.m. A.G.B.	
12-12-14	Started instruction 1. Can. Div. (8 Brigade) in simple trench work (pattern referred to in Tactical Notes issued by H.Q. 1.C.D.) and a few Officers in use of bombs. Interviewed A.G. for A.E. re bomb making and spherical bombs. A.G.B.	
13-12-14.	Instruction begun on 12th continued. A.G.B	
14.12.14.	Instruction cont. with two Regts. but as orders were received to make preparation to move at short notice they returned to lines early. A.G.B.	
16-12-14.	Returned Orders received for instruction in trench work to continue. Heard that 3rd & 7th Indian Divn. can use some of our bombs etc. A.G.B	

WAR DIARY or INTELLIGENCE SUMMARY.

Army Form C. 2118.

(Erase heading not required.)

Instructions regarding War Diaries and Intelligence Summaries are contained in F. S. Regs., Part II, and the Staff Manual respectively. Title pages will be prepared in manuscript.

Hour, Date, Place.	Summary of Events and Information.	Remarks and references to Appendices.
AUCHEL 17-12-14	Experiment in cover for machine gun. Arranged for Lucknow Brigade to continue trench work on 13-12-14. A.G.B	
18-12-14	Work cancelled by G.O.C. Lucknow Brigade on account of rain. A.G.B	
19-12-14	Two Rgts. Lucknow did some work on trenches in rain. Experiment in machine gun pit. A.G.B	
20-12-14	Lecture to Officers of Lucknow Brigade on trench work. Experiment in machine gun emplacement.	
21-12-14	Brought trench mortar from Hallines. A.G.B.	
22-12-14	Recd. orders at 5.15 a.m. to march at once. About 7.0 a.m. orders were modified to march independently at 10.0 a.m. Moved to HAM. A.G.B	
23-12-14 HAM	C.R.E. went to AUCHEL ref. compensation board and to BETHUNE re mortar bombs. A.G.B	
24-12-14	C.R.E and Major Bremner consulted Col. Rawlinson re new trench mortar at MERVILLE. A.G.B ~~Moved to St Hilaire~~	

WAR DIARY
or
INTELLIGENCE SUMMARY.

(Erase heading not required.)

Army Form C. 2118.

Hour, Date, Place.	Summary of Events and Information.	Remarks and references to Appendices.
25-12-14 ST. HILAIRE.	Moved to ST. HILAIRE - A.G.B	
26-12-14.	Compensation Board at AUCHEL (Major Brunner) A.G.B.	
27-12-14.	Compensation Board at AUCHEL. Col. Leslie went to interview G.O.C. re hand bombs - A.G.B	
28-12-14.	Interviewed Chief Engineer Indian Corps re. trench warfare - A.G.B.	
29-12-14.	Lieut. Col. Leslie went to St. Omer and Hallines re. manufacture of spherical bombs - A.G.B	
31-12-14	Between 6.00 p.m and 7.00 p.m. Captain Molesworth R.E. Comdg. 2nd Field Troop, 1st Indian Cavalry Divn. was found dead in his bedroom from a wound accidentally received from his own Pistol - A.G.B	

G.A.Leslie
Lieut Colonel R.E.
D.A.D. Eng. Comdt. 1st I.C.Div.

St. Hilaire - Cettes
1/1/15 -

121/4401

WAR DIARY

of

Senior Engineer Officer, 1st Ind. Cavy. Divn.

From 1-1-1915 To 31-1-1915

Confidential

War Diary
of
Senior Engineer Officer,
1st Indian Cavalry Division

from 1st January 1915, to 31st January 1915

WAR DIARY
or
INTELLIGENCE SUMMARY.

(Erase heading not **required**.)

Army Form C. 2118.

Instructions regarding War Diaries and Intelligence Summaries are contained in F. S. Regs., Part II, and the Staff Manual respectively. Title pages will be prepared in manuscript.

Hour, Date, Place.	Summary of Events and Information.	Remarks and references to Appendices.
St. Hilaire 1-1-15	Captain Molesworth R.E. O/C Field Troop, 1st Indian Cavalry Div'n was buried with military honours in the St Hilaire graveyard at 3.00 p.m. A.B.	
2-1-15	Major Brenner R.E. on compensation board at AIRE(?) - Telegram received from Corps Hd. Qrs. announcing detrainment this morning at ST. OMER of 2/ Field Squadron from England. Lieut O'Neil left for leave in England. A.B.	
3-1-15	A visit to H.Qtrs of 1st & 2nd Indian Cavalry Div'n resulted in finding that the 2nd Field Squadron referred to on 2-1-15 consisted of wheeled transport, horses & drivers for both 1st & 2nd Field Squadrons. They are for present attached to 2nd Indian Cav. Div'n. A.B.	
4-1-15	Arranged for classes in bomb throwing. Making up bombs for classes A.B.	
5-1-15	Classes in bomb throwing. A.B.	
6-1-15	Classes in bomb throwing. Major Brenner on compensation board at AIRE(?) - A.B.	

WAR DIARY
or
INTELLIGENCE SUMMARY.
(Erase heading not required.)

Army Form C. 2118.

Instructions regarding War Diaries and Intelligence Summaries are contained in F. S. Regs., Part II, and the Staff Manual respectively. Title pages will be prepared in manuscript.

Hour, Date, Place.	Summary of Events and Information.	Remarks and references to Appendices.
ST. HILAIRE 7-1-15	Classes in bomb throwing. CRE to HALLINES foundry - brought back 100 cast-iron spherical bombs for bomb gun, also second bomb gun.	
8-1-15	Classes in bomb throwing - RE officers from 2nd Div. who attended. Orders received at 4 PM to despatch Field Troop to report to GOC SIALKOTE Brigade at FESTUBERT. Following details despatched at 5.45 PM. Brit. Officers - Major Brenner RE, Lieut Wickham RE. Indian Officers - 2, B.N.C.Os - 1, Indian N.C.O & Sappers 30, French Interpreter - 1, Gwalior Indian Transport - Indian Officer - 1, Indian R & F - 19, Ponies 36, Tongas 14, Transport Carts 2	

WAR DIARY or INTELLIGENCE SUMMARY.

Army Form C. 2118.

Hour, Date, Place.	Summary of Events and Information.	Remarks and references to Appendices.
9-1-15	Major Bremner reported to G.O.C. SIALKOTE Brigade about 8:00 p.m. on 8.1.15 at FESTUBERT and this morning received orders for work on partially made trenches S.E. of FESTUBERT and about 300x behind our front line trenches. Work began after dark and consisted chiefly of bundle revetment. Work was stopped about 1.30 a.m. on 10.1.15 there being no more bundles. Night was very dark and rainy. Enemy constantly sent up star shells. Rifle fire always slackened while shell was burning but the going out of the light was invariably followed by a burst of fire. Bullets over working party were nearly all high. Party was sniped at from behind our own lines.	
10-1-15	Work same as on 9-1-15. Left billet at 3:00 p.m. commenced work about 5.45 p.m. Ceased work about 12:00 midnight. Night same as 9.1.15. Enemy's rifle fire less than on 9.1.15. Star shell about the same. Enemy used search lights for a short time. Borrowed some Pathans from 30th Cavalry to try to spot snipers who	

WAR DIARY
or
INTELLIGENCE SUMMARY.

(Erase heading not required.)

Army Form C. 2118.

Instructions regarding War Diaries and Intelligence Summaries are contained in F. S. Regs., Part II, and the Staff Manual respectively. Title pages will be prepared in manuscript.

Hour, Date, Place.	Summary of Events and Information.	Remarks and references to Appendices.
10-1-15 (cont)	fired a few shots when we began work. No result but one sentry said he saw a man moving about close to us who he took for one of our men. I am told Enemy shelled this ground shortly after we left it. A.G.B.	
11-1-15	Returned to ST. HILAIRE arriving at 6.20 p.m. Lieut. Chase R.E. reported having joined Field Troop. A.G.B.	
12-1-15	Experiments with bomb mortars. A.G.B.	
13-1-15	do — Col. Leslie to ST. OMER, with A.Q.M.G. Ind. Cav. Corps. A.G.B.	
14-1-15	Accident with bomb mortar. No injuries. Major Brenner exchanged posts with 20th & 21st Coys. S. & M. 3rd Ind. Div. A.G.B.	
15-1-15	Bomb mortar experiments. Field works. Lieut. Chase R.E. returned from temporary duty with Field Troop 2/ I.C. Div. A.G.B.	
16.1.15	Major Shaw R.E. reported arrival in forenoon. Capt. Chase R.E. left for temporary duty with the 2/ British Field Squadron (Ranger). A.G.B.	

WAR DIARY
or
INTELLIGENCE SUMMARY.
(Erase heading not required.)

Army Form O. 2118.

Instructions regarding War Diaries and Intelligence Summaries are contained in F. S. Regs., Part II, and the Staff Manual respectively. Title pages will be prepared in manuscript.

Hour, Date, Place.	Summary of Events and Information.	Remarks and references to Appendices.
18-1-15	Cav. Corps concentration parade at 10.30 a.m.	Adj. B
19-1-15	Workshops, trench work etc.	Adj. B
20-1-15	Lt. Col. G.A. Leslie reported departure on 7 days leave to England in forenoon.	Adj. B
21-1-15	Workshops	Adj. B
22-1-15	Organization of new Field Squadron R.E.	Adj. B
23-1-15	do.	
24-1-15	do. (Corps H.Q.)	Adj. B
25-1-15	do. (G.H.Q)	Adj. B
26-1-15	do. (Corps. H.Q)	Adj. B
	Lieut. Colonel G.A. Leslie reported arrival from leave to England in afternoon.	
27-1-15	Organization of new Field squadron	Adj. B
28-1-15	do. (Clarques)	Adj. B
29-1-15	Field Day, 1st Cav. Div. attended by Lt Col. Leslie. Orders received 10.20 P.M. to be in readiness to move at two hours' notice.	Cav. Cav.
30-1-15	Majors Brenner & Evans temporarily detached to CLARQUES to take over & train personnel & horses belonging to new F. Squadron of 1st Div.	Cav.
31-1-15	Organization of new Field Squadron.	Cav.

G.A. Leslie
Lt Col R.E.
CRE 1st Indian Cav Div

Serial No 50.

121/4719

WAR DIARY OF

Senior Royal Engineer Officer 1st Indian Cavalry Division.

From 1st February 1915 To 28th February 1915.

WAR DIARY or INTELLIGENCE SUMMARY.

Army Form C. 2118.

Instructions regarding War Diaries and Intelligence Summaries are contained in F. S. Regs., Part II, and the Staff Manual respectively. Title pages will be prepared in manuscript.

(Erase heading not required.)

No 3 Section A. G's Office at Base I.E. Force
Passed to _____ S. Sectⁿ
on 4 - 3 - 15

Hour, Date, Place.	Summary of Events and Information.	Remarks and references to Appendices.
1/2/15. St Hilaire	Majors Bremner and Evans RE at CLARQUES taking over Wagons, Horses & Drivers of new RE. Field Squadron for 1st Indⁿ Cav^l Divⁿ. S&M Field Troop doing field works at St Hilaire	G.a.l
2/2/15 "	— Ditto — Capt Chase RE. reported his return from GORRE where he has been working on construction of reserve trenches and Points - d'Appui for the 1st Corps since 16th Jany. French interpreter De Grammont transferred to St OMER.	G.a.l
3/2/15 "	Training of new RE Field Squadron horses & drivers at CLARQUES by Majors Bremner & Evans. Field Works & Wire Entanglements by S&M. Field Troop at St Hilaire.	G.a.l

WAR DIARY
~~or~~
~~INTELLIGENCE SUMMARY.~~

(Erase heading not required.)

Instructions regarding War Diaries and Intelligence Summaries are contained in F. S. Regs., Part II, and the Staff Manual respectively. Title pages will be prepared in manuscript.

Army Form O. 2118.

Hour, Date, Place.	Summary of Events and Information.	Remarks and references to Appendices.
4/2/15. St. Hilaire.	CRE to Iron Foundry at HALLINES to order casting of a stock of cylindrical hand grenades. Order refused owing to press of work & scarcity of labour.	Ctd
5/2/15 "	Approval of A.D.V.S. to Co. C. obtained to transferring horses wagons &c of new RE 7th Squadron (in formation) from CLARQUES to ST HILAIRE. Orders sent to Major Bremner to move tomorrow.	Ctd
7.2.15 "	Two Officers, fifty-one Driver R.E. and eighty six horses with twenty vehicles of 1st Indian Field Squadron R.E. arrived.	Major A.G. Bremner R.E. " W.H. Evans R.E.
8-2-15 "	Squadron and Field Troop employed on treating horses for skin disease &c and overhauling vehicles.	Ctd
10-2-15 "		Ctd
11.2.15 to 13.2.15	Do. do.	Ctd

WAR DIARY
of
INTELLIGENCE SUMMARY.
(Erase heading not required.)

Army Form C. 2118.

Instructions regarding War Diaries and Intelligence Summaries are contained in F. S. Regs., Part II, and the Staff Manual respectively. Title pages will be prepared in manuscript.

Hour, Date, Place.	Summary of Events and Information.	Remarks and references to Appendices.
ST. HILAIRE. 14-2-15	Lieut. Col. Leslie and Captain Cleane left on 7 day leave to England. Horses of 1st Indian Field Squadron suffering from mange, strangles, Catarrh, ring worm etc are improving rapidly. Sound horses being made up into teams. Some difficulty experienced with draught horses not being broken to draught.	Cont
15-2-15	Horses still improving in spite of exceptionally bad weather and having to stand in the open up to their hocks in mud. Horses without rugs have made marked improvement. Men's boots rapidly becoming unserviceable although all were new within 3 months. Do. riding breeches. Making up team etc.	Cont
16-2-15		Cont
17-2-15	5 Drivers sent to Hospital for treatment for itch. Disease brought from CLARQUES.	Cont

WAR DIARY

INTELLIGENCE SUMMARY.

(Erase heading not required.)

Army Form C. 2118.

Instructions regarding War Diaries and Intelligence Summaries are contained in F. S. Regs., Part II, and the Staff Manual respectively. Title pages will be prepared in manuscript.

Hour, Date, Place.	Summary of Events and Information.	Remarks and references to Appendices.
ST. HILAIRE 18-2-15	Routine - Received orders to report to C.R.E. 1st Army.	Cont.
19-2-15	Routine - Major Bremner reported to C.R.E. 1st Army and received orders to meet C.R.E. Meerut Divn.	Cont.
20-2-15	Major Bremner met C.R.E. Meerut Divn. at ROBECQ and arranged work for 1st Ind. Cav. Divn. Fixed sites and nature of work. Lieut. Colonel Leslie returned from leave.	Cont.
21-2-15	Major W. H. Evans proceeded on leave.	Cont.
22-2-15	Major Bremner visited I. Cav. Corps Hd. Quarters re. employing Corps on trench work. Lieut. Col. Leslie also reported to Corps Hd. Quarters re. bomb thrower being made in London by Messrs Bozo & Co. ~~Lieut. Col. Leslie returned from 7 days leave in England~~	Cont.
23-2-15	Lieut. Col. Leslie to G.H.Q. to show photos &c of "Bozo" bomb thrower to Chief Engineer, and to watch experiments with rocket bomb gun. Lieut Wallack - interpreter - proceeded on leave.	Cont.
24-2-15	Trench building in vicinity of ST VENANT with working parties of three regiments of SIALKOTE Brigade begun. This section is part of Reserve Line.	Cont.

WAR DIARY OF INTELLIGENCE SUMMARY.

(Erase heading not required.)

Army Form C. 2118.

Hour, Date, Place.	Summary of Events and Information.	Remarks and references to Appendices.
St HILAIRE 25.2.15	Major Bremner, Capt. Wickham and Indian S+M Field Troop sent to live at St VENANT so as to be near work on Reserve Line of trenches being built by working parties of 1st Cav: Div".	C/al
26.2.15	Lieut: Col: Leslie to St VENANT & back to inspect work on trenches. Work in progress there by 1. I. C. D under direction of Major Bremner	C/al
28.2.15	Instruction in loading & priming projectiles & firing trench mortars given by Lt: Col: Leslie to Officers & NCOs of R.H.A. Batteries.	C/al
N.B.	This diary will be incorporated in that of the R.E. Field Squadron, 1st I.C.D. from 1st March 1915.	G A Leslie Lt Col R.E. C R E 1st Indian Cav Div

www.ingramcontent.com/pod-product-compliance
Lightning Source LLC
Chambersburg PA
CBHW081250170426
4319ICB00037B/2109